Dorothy Lucy

Merry Christmas

1925.

Felix

MAIN STREET AND OTHER POEMS

MAIN STREET

and

OTHER POEMS

by

Joyce Kilmer

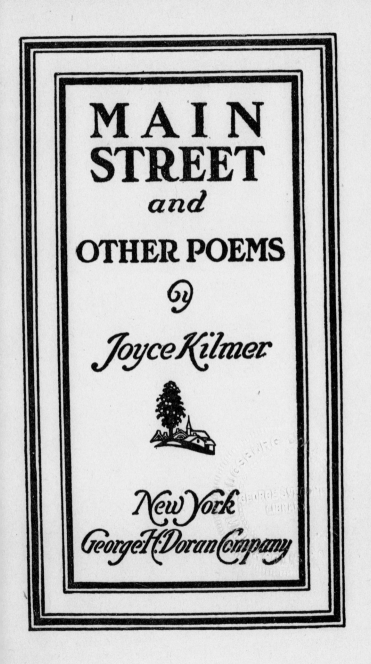

New York

George H. Doran Company

TO
MRS. EDMUND LEAMY

Some of these poems are reprinted by permission, which is hereby gratefully acknowledged, of The Bellman, The Bookman, The Boston Transcript, the Catholic World, Collier's, The Columbiad, Contemporary Verse, The Delineator, Extension, House and Garden, The Magnificat, McBride's Magazine, The National Sunday Magazine, The New Witness, The New York Times, The Outlook, Poetry: a Magazine of Verse, The Poetry Review, The Queen's Work, and Studies.

CONTENTS

CONTENTS

MAIN STREET AND OTHER POEMS

MAIN STREET

(For S. M. L.)

I LIKE to look at the blossomy track of the moon
upon the sea,
But it isn't half so fine a sight as Main Street used
to be
When it all was covered over with a couple of
feet of snow,
And over the crisp and radiant road the ringing
sleighs would go.

Now, Main Street bordered with autumn leaves,
it was a pleasant thing,
And its gutters were gay with dandelions early in
the Spring;
I like to think of it white with frost or dusty in
the heat,
Because I think it is humaner than any other
street.

MAIN STREET (continued)

A city street that is busy and wide is ground by a
      thousand wheels,
And a burden of traffic on its breast is all it ever
      feels:
It is dully conscious of weight and speed and of
      work that never ends,
But it cannot be human like Main Street, and
      recognise its friends.

There were only about a hundred teams on Main
      Street in a day,
And twenty or thirty people, I guess, and some
      children out to play.
And there wasn't a wagon or buggy, or a man or
      a girl or a boy
That Main Street didn't remember, and somehow
      seem to enjoy.

The truck and the motor and trolley car and the
      elevated train
They make the weary city street reverberate with
      pain:

MAIN STREET (continued)

But there is yet an echo left deep down within my
    heart
Of the music the Main Street cobblestones made
    beneath a butcher's cart.

God be thanked for the Milky Way that runs
    across the sky,
That's the path that my feet would tread when-
    ever I have to die.
Some folks call it a Silver Sword, and some a
    Pearly Crown,
But the only thing I think it is, is Main Street,
    Heaventown.

ROOFS

(For Amelia Josephine Burr)

THE road is wide and the stars are out and the
    breath of the night is sweet,
And this is the time when wanderlust should
    seize upon my feet.
But I'm glad to turn from the open road and the
    starlight on my face,
And to leave the splendour of out-of-doors for a
    human dwelling place.

I never have seen a vagabond who really liked to
    roam
All up and down the streets of the world and not
    to have a home:
The tramp who slept in your barn last night and
    left at break of day
Will wander only until he finds another place to
    stay.

ROOFS (continued)

A gypsy-man will sleep in his cart with canvas
    overhead;
Or else he'll go into his tent when it is time for
    bed.
He'll sit on the grass and take his ease so long
    as the sun is high,
But when it is dark he wants a roof to keep away
    the sky.

If you call a gypsy a vagabond, I think you do him
    wrong,
For he never goes a-travelling but he takes his
    home along.
And the only reason a road is good, as every
    wanderer knows,
Is just because of the homes, the homes, the
    homes to which it goes.

They say that life is a highway and its milestones
    are the years,
And now and then there's a toll-gate where you
    buy your way with tears.

ROOFS (continued)

It's a rough road and a steep road and it stretches
    broad and far,
But at last it leads to a golden Town where
    golden Houses are.

THE SNOWMAN IN THE YARD

(For Thomas Augustine Daly)

THE Judge's house has a splendid porch, with
    pillars and steps of stone,
  And the Judge has a lovely flowering hedge
    that came from across the seas;
In the Hales' garage you could put my house and
    everything I own,
  And the Hales have a lawn like an emerald
    and a row of poplar trees.

Now I have only a little house, and only a little
    lot,
  And only a few square yards of lawn, with
    dandelions starred;
But when Winter comes, I have something there
    that the Judge and the Hales have not,
  And it's better worth having than all their
    wealth—it's a snowman in the yard.

THE SNOWMAN IN THE YARD (continued)

The Judge's money brings architects to make his
      mansion fair;
  The Hales have seven gardeners to make their
      roses grow;
The Judge can get his trees from Spain and
      France and everywhere,
  And raise his orchids under glass in the midst
      of all the snow.

But I have something no architect or gardener
      ever made,
  A thing that is shaped by the busy touch of
      little mittened hands:
And the Judge would give up his lonely estate,
      where the level snow is laid
  For the tiny house with the trampled yard, the
      yard where the snowman stands.

They say that after Adam and Eve were driven
      away in tears
  To toil and suffer their life-time through,
      because of the sin they sinned,

THE SNOWMAN IN THE YARD (continued)

The Lord made Winter to punish them for half
their exiled years,
To chill their blood with the snow, and pierce
their flesh with the icy wind.

But we who inherit the primal curse, and labour
for our bread,
Have yet, thank God, the gift of Home, though
Eden's gate is barred:
And through the Winter's crystal veil, Love's
roses blossom red,
For him who lives in a house that has a snow-
man in the yard.

A BLUE VALENTINE

(For Aline)

MONSIGNORE,
        Right Reverend Bishop Valentinus,
Sometime of Interamna, which is called Ferni,
Now of the delightful Court of Heaven,
I respectfully salute you,
I genuflect
And I kiss your episcopal ring.

It is not, Monsignore,
The fragrant memory of your holy life,
Nor that of your shining and joyous martyrdom,
Which causes me now to address you.
But since this is your august festival, Monsignore,
It seems appropriate to me to state
According to a venerable and agreeable custom,
That I love a beautiful lady.
Her eyes, Monsignore,
Are so blue that they put lovely little blue reflec-
    tions

A BLUE VALENTINE (continued)

On everything that she looks at,
Such as a wall
Or the moon
Or my heart.
It is like the light coming through blue stained
    glass,
Yet not quite like it,
For the blueness is not transparent,
Only translucent.
Her soul's light shines through,
But her soul cannot be seen.
It is something elusive, whimsical, tender, wanton,
    infantile, wise
And noble.
She wears, Monsignore, a blue garment,
Made in the manner of the Japanese.
It is very blue—
I think that her eyes have made it more blue,
Sweetly staining it
As the pressure of her body has graciously given
    it form.

A BLUE VALENTINE (continued

Loving her, Monsignore,
I love all her attributes;
But I believe
That even if I did not love her
I would love the blueness of her eyes,
And her blue garment, made in the manner of
    the Japanese.

Monsignore,
I have never before troubled you with a request.
The saints whose ears I chiefly worry with my
    pleas are the most exquisite and maternal
    Brigid,
Gallant Saint Stephen, who puts fire in my blood,
And your brother bishop, my patron,
The generous and jovial Saint Nicholas of Bari.
But, of your courtesy, Monsignore,
Do me this favour:
When you this morning make your way
To the Ivory Throne that bursts into bloom with
    roses because of her who sits upon it,

A BLUE VALENTINE (continued)

When you come to pay your devoir to Our Lady,
I beg you, say to her:
"Madame, a poor poet, one of your singing
    servants yet on earth,
Has asked me to say that at this moment he is
    especially grateful to you
For wearing a blue gown."

HOUSES

(For Aline)

WHEN you shall die and to the sky
  Serenely, delicately go,
Saint Peter, when he sees you there,
  Will clash his keys and say:
"Now talk to her, Sir Christopher!
  And hurry, Michelangelo!
She wants to play at building,
  And you've got to help her play!"

Every architect will help erect
  A palace on a lawn of cloud,
With rainbow beams and a sunset roof,
  And a level star-tiled floor;
And at your will you may use the skill
  Of this gay angelic crowd,
When a house is made you will throw it down,
  And they'll build you twenty more.

HOUSES (continued)

For Christopher Wren and these other men
  Who used to build on earth
Will love to go to work again
  If they may work for you.
"This porch," you'll say, "should go this
      way!"
  And they'll work for all they're worth,
And they'll come to your palace every
      morning,
  And ask you what to do.

And when night comes down on Heaven-town
  (If there should be night up there)
You will choose the house you like the best
  Of all that you can see:
And its walls will glow as you drowsily go
  To the bed up the golden stair,
And I hope you'll be gentle enough to keep
  A room in your house for me.

IN MEMORY

I

SERENE and beautiful and very wise,
   Most erudite in curious Grecian lore,
 You lay and read your learned books, and bore
A weight of unshed tears and silent sighs.
The song within your heart could never rise
   Until love bade it spread its wings and soar.
   Nor could you look on Beauty's face before
A poet's burning mouth had touched your eyes.

Love is made out of ecstasy and wonder;
   Love is a poignant and accustomed pain.
It is a burst of Heaven-shaking thunder;
   It is a linnet's fluting after rain.
Love's voice is through your song; above and
      under
   And in each note to echo and remain.

IN MEMORY (continued)

II

Because Mankind is glad and brave and young,
   Full of gay flames that white and scarlet glow,
   All joys and passions that Mankind may know
By you were nobly felt and nobly sung.
Because Mankind's heart every day is wrung
   By Fate's wild hands that twist and tear it so,
   Therefore you echoed Man's undying woe,
A harp Aeolian on Life's branches hung.

So did the ghosts of toiling children hover
   About the piteous portals of your mind;
Your eyes, that looked on glory, could discover
   The angry scar to which the world was blind:
And it was grief that made Mankind your lover,
   And it was grief that made you love Mankind.

IN MEMORY (continued)

III

Before Christ left the Citadel of Light,
　　To tread the dreadful way of human birth,
　　His shadow sometimes fell upon the earth
And those who saw it wept with joy and fright.
"Thou art Apollo, than the sun more bright!"
　　They cried. "Our music is of little worth,
　　But thrill our blood with thy creative mirth
Thou god of song, thou lord of lyric might!"

O singing pilgrim! who could love and follow
　　Your lover Christ, through even love's despair,
You knew within the cypress-darkened hollow
　　The feet that on the mountain are so fair.
For it was Christ that was your own Apollo,
　　And thorns were in the laurel on your hair.

APOLOGY

(For Eleanor Rogers Cox)

FOR blows on the fort of evil
    That never shows a breach,
For terrible life-long races
    To a goal no foot can reach,
For reckless leaps into darkness
    With hands outstretched to a star.
There is jubilation in Heaven
    Where the great dead poets are.

There is joy over disappointment
    And delight in hopes that were vain.
Each poet is glad there was no cure
    To stop his lonely pain.
For nothing keeps a poet
    In his high singing mood
Like unappeasable hunger
    For unattainable food.

APOLOGY (continued)

So fools are glad of the folly
   That made them weep and sing,
And Keats is thankful for Fanny Brawne
   And Drummond for his king.
They know that on flinty sorrow
   And failure and desire
The steel of their souls was hammered
   To bring forth the lyric fire.

Lord Byron and Shelley and Plunkett,
   McDonough and Hunt and Pearse
See now why their hatred of tyrants
   Was so insistently fierce.
Is Freedom only a Will-o'-the-wisp
   To cheat a poet's eye?
Be it phantom or fact, it's a noble cause
   In which to sing and to die!

So not for the Rainbow taken
   And the magical White Bird snared
The poets sing grateful carols
   In the place to which they have fared;

APOLOGY (continued)

But for their lifetime's passion,
   The quest that was fruitless and long,
They chorus their loud thanksgiving
   To the thorn-crowned Master of Song.

THE PROUD POET

(For Shaemas O Sheel)

ONE winter night a Devil came and sat upon
my bed,
His eyes were full of laughter for his heart was
full of crime.
"Why don't you take up fancy work, or embroi-
dery?" he said,
"For a needle is as manly a tool as a pen that
makes a rhyme!"
"You little ugly Devil," said I, "go back to Hell
For the idea you express I will not listen to:
I have trouble enough with poetry and poverty as
well,
Without having to pay attention to orators like
you.

"When you say of the making of ballads and
songs that it is woman's work
You forget all the fighting poets that have been
in every land.

THE PROUD POET (continued)

There was Byron who left all his lady-loves to
      fight against the Turk,
    And David, the Singing King of the Jews, who
      was born with a sword in his hand.
It was yesterday that Rupert Brooke went out to
      the Wars and died,
    And Sir Philip Sidney's lyric voice was as sweet
      as his arm was strong;
And Sir Walter Raleigh met the axe as a lover
      meets his bride,
    Because he carried in his soul the courage of
      his song.

"And there is no consolation so quickening to the
      heart
    As the warmth and whiteness that come from
      the lines of noble poetry.
It is strong joy to read it when the wounds of the
      spirit smart,
    It puts the flame in a lonely breast where only
      ashes be.

THE PROUD POET (continued)

It is strong joy to read it, and to make it is a
    thing
    That exalts a man with a sacreder pride than
    any pride on earth.
For it makes him kneel to a broken slave and set
    his foot on a king,
    And it shakes the walls of his little soul with
    the echo of God's mirth.

"There was the poet Homer had the sorrow to be
    blind,
    Yet a hundred people with good eyes would
    listen to him all night;
For they took great enjoyment in the heaven of
    his mind,
    And were glad when the old blind poet let them
    share his powers of sight.
And there was Heine lying on his mattress all day
    long,
    He had no wealth, he had no friends, he had no
    joy at all,

THE PROUD POET (continued)

Except to pour his sorrow into little cups of song,
    And the world finds in them the magic wine
        that his broken heart let fall.

"And these are only a couple of names from a list
        of a thousand score
    Who have put their glory on the world in poverty
        and pain.
And the title of poet's a noble thing, worth living
        and dying for,
    Though all the devils on earth and in Hell spit
        at me their disdain.
It is stern work, it is perilous work, to thrust your
        hand in the sun
    And pull out a spark of immortal flame to warm
        the hearts of men:
But Prometheus, torn by the claws and beaks
        whose task is never done,
    Would be tortured another eternity to go
        stealing fire again."

LIONEL JOHNSON

(For the Rev. John J. Burke, C. S. P.)

THERE was a murkier tinge in London's air
　　As if the honest fog blushed black for shame.
　　Fools sang of sin, for other fools' acclaim,
And Milton's wreath was tossed to Baudelaire.
The flowers of evil blossomed everywhere,
　　But in their midst a radiant lily came
　　Candescent, pure, a cup of living flame,
Bloomed for a day, and left the earth more fair

And was it Charles, thy "fair and fatal King,"
　　Who bade thee welcome to the lovely land?
Or did Lord David cease to harp and sing
　　To take in his thine emulative hand?
Or did Our Lady's smile shine forth, to bring
　　Her lyric Knight within her choir to stand?

FATHER GERARD HOPKINS, S. J.

WHY didst thou carve thy speech laboriously,
 And match and blend thy words with
 curious art?
 For Song, one saith, is but a human heart
Speaking aloud, undisciplined and free.
Nay, God be praised, Who fixed thy task for thee!
 Austere, ecstatic craftsman, set apart
 From all who traffic in Apollo's mart,
On thy phrased paten shall the Splendour be!

Now, carelessly we throw a rhyme to God,
 Singing His praise when other songs are done.
But thou, who knewest paths Teresa trod,
 Losing thyself, what is it thou hast won?
O bleeding feet, with peace and glory shod!
 O happy moth, that flew into the Sun!

GATES AND DOORS

(For Richardson Little Wright)

THERE was a gentle hostler
   (And blessèd be his name!)
He opened up the stable
  The night Our Lady came.
Our Lady and Saint Joseph,
  He gave them food and bed,
And Jesus Christ has given him
  A glory round his head.

So let the gate swing open
  However poor the yard,
Lest weary people visit you
  And find their passage barred;
Unlatch the door at midnight
  And let your lantern's glow
Shine out to guide the traveler's feet
  To you across the snow.

GATES AND DOORS (continued)

There was a courteous hostler
    (He is in Heaven to-night)
He held Our Lady's bridle
    And helped her to alight;
He spread clean straw before her
    Whereon she might lie down,
And Jesus Christ has given him
    An everlasting crown.

Unlock the door this evening
    And let your gate swing wide,
Let all who ask for shelter
    Come speedily inside.
What if your yard be narrow?
    What if your house be small?
There is a Guest is coming
    Will glorify it all.

There was a joyous hostler
    Who knelt on Christmas morn
Beside the radiant manger
    Wherein his Lord was born.

GATES AND DOORS (continued)

His heart was full of laughter,
  His soul was full of bliss
When Jesus, on His Mother's lap,
  Gave him His hand to kiss.

Unbar your heart this evening
  And keep no stranger out,
Take from your soul's great portal
  The barrier of doubt.
To humble folk and weary
  Give hearty welcoming,
Your breast shall be to-morrow
  The cradle of a King.

THE ROBE OF CHRIST

(For Cecil Chesterton)

AT the foot of the Cross on Calvary
   Three soldiers sat and diced,
And one of them was the Devil
   And he won the Robe of Christ.

When the Devil comes in his proper form
   To the chamber where I dwell,
I know him and make the Sign of the Cross
   Which drives him back to Hell.

And when he comes like a friendly man
   And puts his hand in mine,
The fervour in his voice is not
   From love or joy or wine.

And when he comes like a woman,
   With lovely, smiling eyes,
Black dreams float over his golden head
   Like a swarm of carrion flies.

THE ROBE OF CHRIST (continued)

Now many a million tortured souls
    In his red halls there be:
Why does he spend his subtle craft
    In hunting after me?

Kings, queens and crested warriors
    Whose memory rings through time,
These are his prey, and what to him
    Is this poor man of rhyme,

That he, with such laborious skill,
    Should change from rôle to rôle,
Should daily act so many a part
    To get my little soul?

Oh, he can be the forest,
    And he can be the sun,
Or a buttercup, or an hour of rest
    When the weary day is done.

I saw him through a thousand veils,
    And has not this sufficed?
Now, must I look on the Devil robed
    In the radiant Robe of Christ?

THE ROBE OF CHRIST (continued)

He comes, and his face is sad and mild,
    With thorns his head is crowned;
There are great bleeding wounds in his feet,
    And in each hand a wound.

How can I tell, who am a fool,
    If this be Christ or no?
Those bleeding hands outstretched to me!
    Those eyes that love me so!

I see the Robe—I look—I hope—
    I fear—but there is one
Who will direct my troubled mind;
    Christ's Mother knows her Son.

O Mother of Good Counsel, lend
    Intelligence to me!
Encompass me with wisdom,
    Thou Tower of Ivory!

"This is the Man of Lies," she says,
    "Disguised with fearful art:
He has the wounded hands and feet,
    But not the wounded heart."

THE ROBE OF CHRIST (continued)

Beside the Cross on Calvary
   She watched them as they diced.
She saw the Devil join the game
   And win the Robe of Christ.

THE SINGING GIRL

(For the Rev. Edward F. Garesché, S. J.)

THERE was a little maiden
    In blue and silver drest,
She sang to God in Heaven
    And God within her breast.

It flooded me with pleasure,
    It pierced me like a sword,
When this young maiden sang: "My soul
    Doth magnify the Lord."

The stars sing all together
    And hear the angels sing,
But they said they had never heard
    So beautiful a thing.

Saint Mary and Saint Joseph,
    And Saint Elizabeth,
Pray for us poets now
    And at the hour of death.

THE ANNUNCIATION

(For Helen Parry Eden)

HAIL Mary, full of grace," the Angel saith.
Our Lady bows her head, and is ashamed;
She has a Bridegroom Who may not be named,
Her mortal flesh bears Him Who conquers death.
Now in the dust her spirit grovelleth;
Too bright a Sun before her eyes has flamed,
Too fair a herald joy too high proclaimed,
And human lips have trembled in God's breath.

O Mother-Maid, thou art ashamed to cover
With thy white self, whereon no stain can be,
Thy God, Who came from Heaven to be thy Lover,
Thy God, Who came from Heaven to dwell in
thee.
About thy head celestial legions hover,
Chanting the praise of thy humility.

ROSES

(For Katherine Brègy)

I WENT to gather roses and twine them in a
　　ring,
For I would make a posy, a posy for the King.
I got an hundred roses, the loveliest there be,
From the white rose vine and the pink rose bush
　　and from the red rose tree.

But when I took my posy and laid it at His feet
I found He had His roses a million times more
　　sweet.
There was a scarlet blossom upon each foot and
　　hand,
And a great pink rose bloomed from His side for
　　the healing of the land.

Now of this fair and awful King there is this
　　marvel told,
That He wears a crown of linkèd thorns instead
　　of one of gold.

ROSES (continued)

Where there are thorns are roses, and I saw a
line of red,
A little wreath of roses around His radiant head.

A red rose is His Sacred Heart, a white rose is
His face,
And His breath has turned the barren world to a
rich and flowery place.
He is the Rose of Sharon, His gardener am I,
And I shall drink His fragrance in Heaven when
I die.

THE VISITATION

(For Louise Imogen Guiney)

THERE is a wall of flesh before the eyes
    Of John, who yet perceives and hails his
    King.
  It is Our Lady's painful bliss to bring
Before mankind the Glory of the skies.
Her cousin feels her womb's sweet burden rise
    And leap with joy, and she comes forth to sing,
    With trembling mouth, her words of welcoming.
She knows her hidden God, and prophesies.

Saint John, pray for us, weary souls that tarry
    Where life is withered by sin's deadly breath.
Pray for us, whom the dogs of Satan harry,
    Saint John, Saint Anne, and Saint Elizabeth.
And, Mother Mary, give us Christ to carry
    Within our hearts, that we may conquer death.

MULTIPLICATION

(For S. M. E.)

I TAKE my leave, with sorrow, of Him I love so
    well;
I look my last upon His small and radiant prison-
    cell;
O happy lamp! to serve Him with never ceasing
    light!
O happy flame! to tremble forever in His sight!

I leave the holy quiet for the loudly human train,
And my heart that He has breathed upon is filled
    with lonely pain.
O King, O Friend, O Lover! What sorer grief
    can be
In all the reddest depths of Hell than banishment
    from Thee?

But from my window as I speed across the sleep-
    ing land
I see the towns and villages wherein His houses
    stand.

MULTIPLICATION (continued)

Above the roofs I see a cross outlined against the
    night,
And I know that there my Lover dwells in His
    sacramental might.

Dominions kneel before Him, and Powers kiss
    His feet,
Yet for me He keeps His weary watch in the
    turmoil of the street:
The King of Kings awaits me, wherever I may go,
O who am I that He should deign to love and
    serve me so?

THANKSGIVING

(For John Bunker)

THE roar of the world is in my ears.
    Thank God for the roar of the world!
Thank God for the mighty tide of fears
    Against me always hurled!

Thank God for the bitter and ceaseless strife,
    And the sting of His chastening rod!
Thank God for the stress and the pain of life,
    And Oh, thank God for God!

THE THORN

(For the Rev. Charles L. O'Donnell, C. S. C.)

THE garden of God is a radiant place,
    And every flower has a holy face:
Our Lady like a lily bends above the cloudy
        sod,
But Saint Michael is the thorn on the rose-
        bush of God.

David is the song upon God's lips,
And Our Lady is the goblet that He sips:
And Gabriel's the breath of His command,
But Saint Michael is the sword in God's right
        hand.

The Ivory Tower is fair to see,
And may her walls encompass me!
But when the Devil comes with the thunder
        of his might,
Saint Michael, show me how to fight!

THE BIG TOP

THE boom and blare of the big brass band is
cheering to my heart
    And I like the smell of the trampled grass and
elephants and hay.
I take off my hat to the acrobat with his delicate,
strong art,
    And the motley mirth of the chalk-faced clown
drives all my care away.

I wish I could feel as they must feel, these players
brave and fair,
    Who nonchalantly juggle death before a staring
throng.
It must be fine to walk a line of silver in the air
    And to cleave a hundred feet of space with a
gesture like a song.

Sir Henry Irving never knew a keener, sweeter
thrill
    Than that which stirs the breast of him who
turns his painted face

THE BIG TOP (continued)

To the circling crowd who laugh aloud and clap
    hands with a will
  As a tribute to the clown who won the great
    wheel-barrow race.

Now, one shall work in the living rock with a
    mallet and a knife,
  And another shall dance on a big white horse
    that canters round a ring,
By another's hand shall colours stand in similitude
    of life;
  And the hearts of the three shall be moved by
    one mysterious high thing.

For the sculptor and the acrobat and the painter
    are the same.
  They know one hope, one fear, one pride, one
    sorrow and one mirth,
And they take delight in the endless fight for the
    fickle world's acclaim;
  For they worship art above the clouds and
    serve her on the earth.

THE BIG TOP (continued)

But you, who can build of the stubborn rock no
form of loveliness,
Who can never mingle the radiant hues to
make a wonder live,
Who can only show your little woe to the world in
a rhythmic dress—
What kind of a counterpart of you does the
three-ring circus give?

Well—here in the little side-show tent to-day
some people stand,
One is a giant, one a dwarf, and one has a
figured skin,
And each is scarred and seared and marred by
Fate's relentless hand,
And each one shows his grief for pay, with a
sort of pride therein.

You put your sorrow into rhyme and want the
world to look;
You sing the news of your ruined hope and
want the world to hear;

THE BIG TOP (continued)

Their woe is pent in a canvas tent and yours in a
      printed book.
  O, poet of the broken heart, salute your
      brothers here!

QUEEN ELIZABETH SPEAKS

MY hands were stained with blood, my heart
    was proud and cold,
My soul is black with shame . . . but I gave
    Shakespeare gold.
So after æons of flame, I may, by grace of God,
Rise up to kiss the dust that Shakespeare's feet
    have trod.

MID-OCEAN IN WAR-TIME

(For My Mother)

THE fragile splendour of the level sea,
  The moon's serene and silver-veilèd face,
 Make of this vessel an enchanted place
Full of white mirth and golden sorcery.
Now, for a time, shall careless laughter be
  Blended with song, to lend song sweeter grace,
  And the old stars, in their unending race,
Shall heed and envy young humanity.

And yet to-night, a hundred leagues away,
  These waters blush a strange and awful red.
Before the moon, a cloud obscenely grey
  Rises from decks that crash with flying lead.
And these stars smile their immemorial way
  On waves that shroud a thousand newly dead!

IN MEMORY OF RUPERT BROOKE

IN alien earth, across a troubled sea,
   His body lies that was so fair and young.
  His mouth is stopped, with half his songs
     unsung;
His arm is still, that struck to make men free.
But let no cloud of lamentation be
   Where, on a warrior's grave, a lyre is hung.
   We keep the echoes of his golden tongue,
We keep the vision of his chivalry.

So Israel's joy, the loveliest of kings,
   Smote now his harp, and now the hostile horde.
To-day the starry roof of Heaven rings
   With psalms a soldier made to praise his Lord;
And David rests beneath Eternal wings,
   Song on his lips, and in his hand a sword.

THE NEW SCHOOL

(For My Mother)

THE halls that were loud with the merry tread
    of young and careless feet
  Are still with a stillness that is too drear to
    seem like holiday,
And never a gust of laughter breaks the calm of
    the dreaming street
  Or rises to shake the ivied walls and frighten
    the doves away.

The dust is on book and on empty desk, and the
    tennis-racquet and balls
  Lie still in their lonely locker and wait for a
    game that is never played,
And over the study and lecture-room and the
    river and meadow falls
  A stern peace, a strange peace, a peace that
    War has made.

THE NEW SCHOOL (continued)

For many a youthful shoulder now is gay with an
epaulet,
And the hand that was deft with a cricket-bat
is defter with a sword,
And some of the lads will laugh to-day where the
trench is red and wet,
And some will win on the bloody field the
accolade of the Lord.

They have taken their youth and mirth away
from the study and playing-ground
To a new school in an alien land beneath an
alien sky;
Out in the smoke and roar of the fight their
lessons and games are found,
And they who were learning how to live are
learning how to die.

And after the golden day has come and the war is
at an end,
A slab of bronze on the chapel wall will tell of
the noble dead.

THE NEW SCHOOL (continued)

And every name on that radiant list will be the
    name of a friend,
  A name that shall through the centuries in
    grateful prayers be said.

And there will be ghosts in the old school, brave
    ghosts with laughing eyes,
  On the field with a ghostly cricket-bat, by the
    stream with a ghostly rod;
They will touch the hearts of the living with a
    flame that sanctifies,
  A flame that they took with strong young hands
    from the altar-fires of God.

EASTER WEEK

(In memory of Joseph Mary Plunkett)

(*"Romantic Ireland's dead and gone,
It's with O'Leary in the grave."*)

WILLIAM BUTLER YEATS.

"ROMANTIC Ireland's dead and gone,
 It's with O'Leary in the grave."
Then, Yeats, what gave that Easter dawn
 A hue so radiantly brave?

There was a rain of blood that day,
 Red rain in gay blue April weather.
It blessed the earth till it gave birth
 To valour thick as blooms of heather.

Romantic Ireland never dies!
 O'Leary lies in fertile ground,
And songs and spears throughout the years
 Rise up where patriot graves are found.

Immortal patriots newly dead
 And ye that bled in bygone years,
What banners rise before your eyes?
 What is the tune that greets your ears?

EASTER WEEK (continued)

The young Republic's banners smile
    For many a mile where troops convene.
O'Connell Street is loudly sweet
    With strains of Wearing of the Green.

The soil of Ireland throbs and glows
    With life that knows the hour is here
To strike again like Irishmen
    For that which Irishmen hold dear.

Lord Edward leaves his resting place
    And Sarsfield's face is glad and fierce.
See Emmet leap from troubled sleep
    To grasp the hand of Padraic Pearse!

There is no rope can strangle song
    And not for long death takes his toll.
No prison bars can dim the stars
    Nor quicklime eat the living soul.

Romantic Ireland is not old.
    For years untold her youth will shine.
Her heart is fed on Heavenly bread,
    The blood of martyrs is her wine.

THE CATHEDRAL OF RHEIMS

(From the French of Émile Verhaeren)

HE who walks through the meadows of Cham-
  pagne
    At noon in Fall, when leaves like gold appear,
    Sees it draw near
Like some great mountain set upon the plain,
From radiant dawn until the close of day,
    Nearer it grows
    To him who goes
Across the country.   When tall towers lay
    Their shadowy pall
    Upon his way,
    He enters, where
The solid stone is hollowed deep by all
Its centuries of beauty and of prayer.

Ancient French temple! thou whose hundred kings
Watch over thee, emblazoned on thy walls,
Tell me, within thy memory-hallowed halls
What chant of triumph, or what war-song rings?

THE CATHEDRAL OF RHEIMS (continued)

Thou hast known Clovis and his Frankish train,
Whose mighty hand Saint Remy's hand did keep
And in thy spacious vault perhaps may sleep
An echo of the voice of Charlemagne.
For God thou has known fear, when from His side
Men wandered, seeking alien shrines and new,
But still the sky was bountiful and blue
And thou wast crowned with France's love and
        pride.
Sacred thou art, from pinnacle to base;
And in thy panes of gold and scarlet glass
The setting sun sees thousandfold his face;
Sorrow and joy, in stately silence pass
Across thy walls, the shadow and the light;
Around thy lofty pillars, tapers white
Illuminate, with delicate sharp flames,
The brows of saints with venerable names,
And in the night erect a fiery wall.
A great but silent fervour burns in all
Those simple folk who kneel, pathetic, dumb,
And know that down below, beside the Rhine—

THE CATHEDRAL OF RHEIMS (continued)

Cannon, horses, soldiers, flags in line—
With blare of trumpets, mighty armies come.

Suddenly, each knows fear;
Swift rumours pass, that every one must hear,
The hostile banners blaze against the sky
And by the embassies mobs rage and cry.
Now war has come, and peace is at an end.
On Paris town the German troops descend.
They are turned back, and driven to Champagne.
And now, as to so many weary men,
The glorious temple gives them welcome, when
It meets them at the bottom of the plain.

At once, they set their cannon in its way.
        There is no gable now, nor wall
That does not suffer, night and day,
        As shot and shell in crushing torrents fall.
The stricken tocsin quivers through the tower;
        The triple nave, the apse, the lonely choir
Are circled, hour by hour,
        With thundering bands of fire
And Death is scattered broadcast among men.

THE CATHEDRAL OF RHEIMS (continued)

And then
That which was splendid with baptismal grace;
The stately arches soaring into space,
The transepts, columns, windows gray and gold,
The organ, in whose tones the ocean rolled,
The crypts, of mighty shades the dwelling places,
The Virgin's gentle hands, the Saints' pure faces,
All, even the pardoning hands of Christ the Lord
Were struck and broken by the wanton sword
Of sacrilegious lust.

O beauty slain, O glory in the dust!
Strong walls of faith, most basely overthrown!
The crawling flames, like adders glistening
Ate the white fabric of this lovely thing.
Now from its soul arose a piteous moan,
The soul that always loved the just and fair.
Granite and marble loud their woe confessed,
The silver monstrances that Popes had blessed,
The chalices and lamps and crosiers rare
Were seared and twisted by a flaming breath;
The horror everywhere did range and swell,

THE CATHEDRAL OF RHEIMS (continued)

The guardian Saints into this furnace fell,
Their bitter tears and screams were stilled in
       death.

Around the flames armed hosts are skirmishing,
The burning sun reflects the lurid scene;
The German army, fighting for its life,
Rallies its torn and terrified left wing;
    And, as they near this place
    The imperial eagles see
    Before them in their flight,
Here, in the solemn night,
The old cathedral, to the years to be
    Showing, with wounded arms, their own
       disgrace.

KINGS

(For the Rev. James B. Dollard)

THE Kings of the earth are men of might,
  And cities are burned for their delight,
And the skies rain death in the silent night,
  And the hills belch death all day!

But the King of Heaven, Who made them all,
Is fair and gentle, and very small;
He lies in the straw, by the oxen's stall—
  Let them think of Him to-day!

THE WHITE SHIPS AND THE RED

(For Alden March)

WITH drooping sail and pennant
  That never a wind may reach,
They float in sunless waters
  Beside a sunless beach.
Their mighty masts and funnels
  Are white as driven snow,
And with a pallid radiance
  Their ghostly bulwarks glow.

Here is a Spanish galleon
  That once with gold was gay,
Here is a Roman trireme
  Whose hues outshone the day.
But Tyrian dyes have faded,
  And prows that once were bright
With rainbow stains wear only
  Death's livid. dreadful white.

THE WHITE SHIPS AND THE RED (continued)

White as the ice that clove her
    That unforgotten day,
Among her pallid sisters
    The grim Titanic lay.
And through the leagues above her
    She looked aghast, and said:
"What is this living ship that comes
    Where every ship is dead?"

The ghostly vessels trembled
    From ruined stern to prow;
What was this thing of terror
    That broke their vigil now?
Down through the startled ocean
    A mighty vessel came,
Not white, as all dead ships must be,
    But red, like living flame!

The pale green waves about her
    Were swiftly, strangely dyed,
By the great scarlet stream that flowed
    From out her wounded side.

THE WHITE SHIPS AND THE RED (continued)

And all her decks were scarlet
    And all her shattered crew.
She sank among the white ghost ships
    And stained them through and through.

The grim *Titanic* greeted her
    "And who art thou?" she said;
"Why dost thou join our ghostly fleet
    Arrayed in living red?
We are the ships of sorrow
    Who spend the weary night,
Until the dawn of Judgment Day,
    Obscure and still and white."

"Nay," said the scarlet visitor,
    "Though I sink through the sea,
A ruined thing that was a ship,
    I sink not as did ye.
For ye met with your destiny
    By storm or rock or fight,
So through the lagging centuries
    Ye wear your robes of white.

THE WHITE SHIPS AND THE RED (continued)

"But never crashing iceberg
　Nor honest shot of foe,
Nor hidden reef has sent me
　The way that I must go.
My wound that stains the waters,
　My blood that is like flame,
Bear witness to a loathly deed,
　A deed without a name.

"I went not forth to battle,
　I carried friendly men,
The children played about my decks,
　The women sang—and then—
And then—the sun blushed scarlet
　And Heaven hid its face,
The world that God created
　Became a shameful place!

"My wrong cries out for vengeance,
　The blow that sent me here
Was aimed in Hell.　My dying scream
　Has reached Jehovah's ear.

THE WHITE SHIPS AND THE RED (continued)

Not all the seven oceans
   Shall wash away that stain;
Upon a brow that wears a crown
   I am the brand of Cain."

When God's great voice assembles
   The fleet on Judgment Day,
The ghosts of ruined ships will rise
   In sea and strait and bay.
Though they have lain for ages
   Beneath the changeless flood,
They shall be white as silver,
   But one—shall be like blood.